Title: Why Do I Have To Be So Tall?
Author: Karen L. Nourse
Illustrated by: Al Margolis

No part of this publication may be reproduced in any form without prior permission in writing from the author.
For additional copies of this book visit: www.amazon.com

©2015 Karen L. Nourse
All rights reserved.

ISBN Paper Book: 978-0-692-56245-1

Library of Congress Control Number: 2015911891

Karen L. Nourse
Publisher
Printed in the USA

For Lilly and Elodie, anything is possible, love you

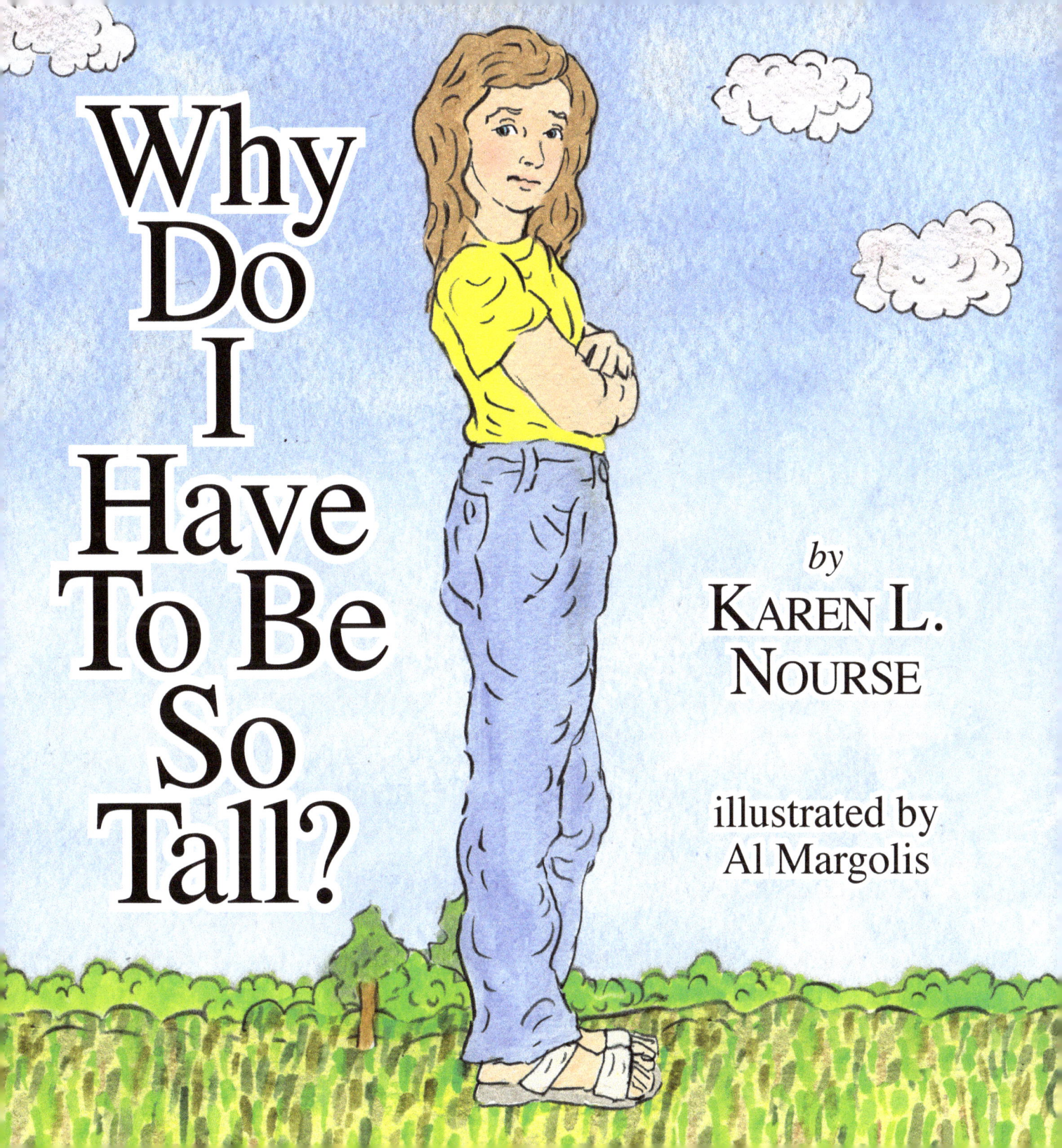

Tina is a girl who is very tall for her age. She is taller than all her classmates, and that even includes all the boys. Sometimes she wishes she were just a little shorter. Then she wouldn't tower over everyone like she does. Tina is eight years old, but she looks like she's ten.

When Tina and her mom go to the shoe store, the clerk always remarks on how big Tina's feet are for her age. She feels like a giraffe whenever he says that.

Tina has an older sister, Lilly, and Tina is even taller than she is. "Why can't I be small like Lilly and the rest of my friends?" asks Tina.

Tina takes after her father. Her mother is average height, but her father is a very tall man.

No matter how hard she tries, she can't get used to being taller than the rest of the kids. Her mom and dad try to tell her that being tall is a wonderful gift.

"You can reach things the other, shorter kids can't reach, and you can run fast because you have longer legs," says Mom.

Tina thinks, *They say that I should be happy I'm tall. Why don't I feel that way?*

It's even hard to find clothes to fit when you are tall. Tina always ends up with pants and shirt sleeves that are too short.

Tina thinks, *Sometimes I wish that I could just sit all the time and never have to get up! When I sit down, I'm not that much bigger than the rest of the kids.*

Every day after school, Tina goes over to her grandma and grandpa's house; they live next door. Grandma always has some homemade soup waiting for her, and Tina looks forward to these visits.

After Tina finishes her soup, Grandpa plays board games with her. Grandma and Grandpa never mention Tina's height to her. Tina loves that.

One day after school, Tina is walking to her grandparents' house when John, a neighbor, asks if she wants to play kickball with his friends.

At first she doesn't want to play, because she thinks she would feel funny running with her long legs. But he keeps insisting she play, so she decides to give it a try.

Tina follows John to his backyard, where all the kids on the team are waiting. Once they meet Tina, they discover that they really like her, and she really likes them.

The team chooses Tina to go first. Before she can say a word, John takes her to home plate and wishes her luck. That's when Tina starts to get nervous. She's afraid she won't be a good kicker or a good runner.

While she's thinking this, she happens to look up, and to her surprise, the pitcher is already rolling the ball to her.

Tina vows, right then and there, to kick the ball as hard as she can—which is exactly what she does. Not only does she kick the ball hard, but she also runs like the wind to first base. All the kids on Tina's team cheer for her. Tina even surprises herself at how fast she can run.

From that moment forward, Tina is not afraid to play. She plays kickball with her team for about an hour and has the best time. At the end of the game, her team wins.

When the game is over, all the kids come up to Tina and tell her how good she is. They even say that she is their best player. John, who is the captain of the team, asks her if she will stay on their team as a forever player. Tina tells John that she will. John says he is glad she is officially on the team. Tina smiles, says thanks, and then says she has to go home.

Tina runs home as fast as she can; she wants to tell her grandparents the good news.

When Tina gets to her grandparents' house, she flings open their front door and tells them everything. "I'm sorry I'm late, but I found out today the kids want me to be on their kickball team. We played one game, and they told me I'm their best player. I also found out that I love playing kickball, and I really like my new friends."

"We're glad to hear you love playing kickball, and we're proud of you," says Grandma, "but please let us know when you will be late next time."

"OK, Grandma, I will."

At dinnertime Tina goes home and tells her parents the good news. Her mom and dad are very happy for her. They all agree to make a special dinner to celebrate Tina joining the kickball team and being their best player.

Later that day, Tina sits down on her bed and thinks of all the things she can do because she is tall. She can reach things her friends can't reach, she can help her teacher erase the high spots on the blackboard, and she can run fast with her long legs.

She thinks, *I guess Mom and Dad were right; being tall can make things easier. It's a good thing I gave kickball a chance, because I would have never known I was such a good player if I hadn't tried. I like being tall!*

About the author

Karen L. Nourse lives with her husband in Connecticut, where she works as an administrative assistant for a university. Together they have three children and two grandchildren, and she loves writing children's books.

About the illustrator

Al Margolis specializes in humorous illustration. His work has been used for both advertising and children's books. Helping children enjoy, learn, and understand their experiences is an important part of his work. Many more examples of his art can be seen at www.almargolis.com.

www.ingramcontent.com/pod-product-compliance
Lightning Source LLC
Chambersburg PA
CBHW061816290426
44110CB00026B/2886